CATHY
WILKES

TATE LIVERPOOL
LENTOS KUNSTMUSEUM LINZ
MUSEUM ABTEIBERG MÖNCHENGLADBACH

This book accompanies the largest and most comprehensive display of Cathy Wilkes' work to date. Bringing together recent installations with works from up to a decade earlier, the exhibition documents the richness and depth of Wilkes' practice. This project is not simply a survey of Wilkes' career tracing the development of her practice. Instead, individual works are combined, overlapped, and particular parts selected and repurposed, to create an overarching installation that stands as an entirely new endeavour, turning fragments from different periods of Wilkes' production into a single total work of art only existing for the duration of this exhibition and its tour. Major installations of recent years, including Untitled 2014 (Tramway, 2014) and Untitled (Possil, at last) 2013 (originally commissioned for the 55th Venice Biennale) are shown inter-connected to elements selected from earlier works. In this sense, the display of Wilkes' art takes on the installation and combinatory procedures that make her practice so mysteriously distinctive. A deep understanding of spatial relationships and the senses of presence and absence that can emanate from objects runs through Wilkes' highly considered and subtle work. Visitors to the exhibition may find themselves in the role of an actor negotiating a theatrical set in which they are suddenly a key character, or perhaps rather an archaeologist excavating fragments from which one might attempt to decipher a lost civilisation, its mythology and social and economic structures.

Often Wilkes' work has been described as uncompromisingly introspective. Her installations originate and are firmly located in linear time and space; as such they are akin to time machines, transporting author and viewers alike to a definite time. They emerge from preoccupations, thoughts, real situations and emotional states of a certain period of Wilkes' life. The composition of objects, their relations, their mysterious evocations and the sets of volumes and voids that make up the theatrical sets are the result – perhaps even the resolution – of the elaboration of a nucleus of affects and ideas, a sort of dream work (Traumarbeit) unravelled in three dimensions. For this reason an exhibition that looks at works from different periods over the past decade involves, for Wilkes, going back to past moments, literally activating a 'retrospective gaze' that not only selects works but effectively reactivates them. The theatricality of her work also comes to the fore in this aspect: the scenes we are presented with are frozen but, reinstalled, the theatre play starts again and the scene changes.

Such metaphorical 'bringing back to life' is not just an emotional experience but part of Wilkes' art, for her works are not necessarily finished and 'set in stone' once they are sent into the world. In fact, a number of them have been modified and reworked when installed again. For example the installation Non Verbal, various dates, has manifested in different versions across time. Such characteristics make her works living organisms evolving organically and expanding in relation to changes in their environment. While museums normally try to fix reality in order to conserve a stable object so that it can be experienced by future generations, this exhibition embraces the instability of Wilkes' practice and makes it its 'condition of possibility': what Immanuel Kant defined as the necessary preconditions for some entity to be able to be experienced. This approach involves abandoning the traditional format of the survey show that requires the finest selection of objects exemplary of a specific practice, instead developing an exhibition framework that reflects what Will Bradley identified as the core of Wilkes' work: 'an attempt to engage with a system of objects in full knowledge of the complex meanings and relationships such a system can produce'.[1]

This openness to re-elaboration, when replicated into the curatorial process, involves rewriting the past rather than just exposing it, bringing art history to a time/space short circuit. The dividing line between works created in distant time dissolves, a parallel universe is set up where past and present are simultaneous. Wilkes has previously mentioned that for her 'life and death are not separated'. The co-penetration of works that takes place in this show implies a similar recognition of boundaries as thresholds, doors to be opened rather than kept closed. Providing the framework for elements from different eras to be brought together into a single galaxy with its own equilibrium and gravitational tension, in this show Wilkes employs metal grids as rigid supports and threaded wool to form supple organic webs instead of walls. These elements inhabit a duplicitous state, as framing and delimiting display mechanisms as well as connecting devices to knit together parts – simultaneously separating and joining disparate elements, while also allowing light to move through a complex structure.

During the conception of this project, and also in the first of the two texts that she publishes in this book, Wilkes has talked about her work as an encouragement to look. The particular intensity of the apprehension that happens when we look is guided by a three-dimensional musical score that aims at generating an awareness of the judgments that we might project onto the world before even decoding it. Her works are frameworks designed to enable a specific way of paying attention. There is a balance between obstruction and facilitation in the way her installations are set up: the feeling that an element is missing from the composition might be deliberately conceived to create a sense of loss. This absence might be the necessary posture to re-tune our attention and our ability to visualise beyond the confines of the visible. The articulation of space between objects can serve as the gap that allows meaning to emerge. Paradoxically, her work is much more musical than three-dimensional. It incorporates change that affects the appearance of the assembled objects, but it also incorporates the time in which the audience's gaze fluctuates, a dance that decodes the artworks both with the senses and the brain. The generation of meaning and emotional engagement is what the artist requires her viewers to perform, like the analysts of a dream that is presented in front of them.

In order to mirror this unique approach, which subverts the conventions of the survey show, this publication is not a conventional catalogue but rather a map and a guide designed to provide further glimpses into Wilkes' working practices and thinking processes. Conceived by the artist working closely with designer Yvonne Quirmbach, the book brings together new texts, photographs of installation details, paintings and new drawings to further expand and develop notions within the show. Like many of her projects, this exhibition is a careful orchestration of objects exposed as a concatenation of selected fragments. The publication reiterates such concerns, highlighting repeated motifs and correspondences in its rhythmical sequence of images and voids. For example the resonance between painted apples and a figure's felt head, the marks on the historical found fabrics employed to dress the figures and their intense investigative looking postures, are just some of the threads recurring in the publication's visual and musical phrases. In this way it acts as a structure to understand Wilkes' practice as a film developing in time and space.

Cathy Wilkes was originally invited to conceive this exhibition at Tate Liverpool by former Head of Exhibitions and Displays Gavin Delahunty (Hoffman Family Senior Curator of Contemporary Art, Dallas Museum of Art) alongside former Assistant Curator Eleanor Clayton (Curator, Hepworth Wakefield). We would like to express our gratitude to them, alongside the dedicated staff at Tate Liverpool in particular Lauren Barnes, Assistant Curator for the incredible vision and rigour she has brought into the project; Tamsin Dillon, Interim Head of Exhibitions and Displays, Sivan Amar, Registrar and Production Manager, Ken Simons, Art Handling Manager and Barry Bentley, Deputy Art Handling Manager for the care and precision they dedicated to such a complex installation as well as Jemima Pyne, Head of Media and Audiences, and Mike Pinnington, Content Editor for their assistance in communicating this project to our audiences. More than a typical touring show, the exhibition's layout is conceived afresh with the artist at each location, and restaged in relation to each new context. At Lentos Kunstmuseum, we would like to thank the entire committed team, in particular Magnus Hofmüller, Head of Production, Andreas Strohhammer, Art Handling Manager, Milena Dimitrova, Registrar, Dunja Schneider, Head of Art Education, and Nina Kirsch, Media and Public Relations. At Museum Abteiberg we would like to thank all our staff for overseeing the restaging of the exhibition with such engagement and care, especially Christine Adolphs, Conservator, Achim Hirdes, Exhibition Technician, and the installation team.

We are deeply grateful to the public museums and private individuals who have so generously lent works from their collections to be part of the exhibition in Liverpool, Linz and Mönchengladbach, in particular the Rennie Collection, who have also supported the exhibition. The exhibition in Tate Liverpool is supported by The Henry Moore Foundation, Culture Ireland and British Council Northern Ireland, to whom we are very grateful. In Liverpool, the exhibition has been made possible by the provision of insurance through the UK Government Indemnity Scheme, and Tate Liverpool would like to thank HM Government for providing Government Indemnity and the Department for Culture, Media and Sport and Arts Council England for arranging the indemnity of works. Museum Abteiberg is deeply grateful to the institutional supporters, the Arts Foundation of North Rhine-Westphalia, and the Hans Fries Foundation who made this exhibition possible in Mönchengladbach.

For her inspired and deeply collaborative approach to the design of this publication, we thank Yvonne Quirmbach, who has worked very closely with Cathy Wilkes to make a book that is highly sensitive to the artist's own vision. We would like to offer our particular thanks to Toby Webster and Xavier Hufkens for generously supporting this publication. Thanks are also due to the teams at The Modern Institute and Xavier Hufkens, who have assisted with many crucial aspects of the exhibition and book with efficiency and diligence throughout. Exceptional thanks are due to

Darren Rhymes who, as assistant to Cathy Wilkes, has supported the entire project from beginning to end with the utmost care and attention. Finally, we would like to offer our deepest debt of gratitude to Cathy Wilkes. The opportunity to temporarily enter her world through this process is an incredible privilege – and one that we are very fortunate to be able to share through this exhibition and book.

Andrea Nixon, Executive Director, Tate Liverpool
Francesco Manacorda, Artistic Director, Tate Liverpool
Stella Rollig, Director, Lentos Kunstmuseum Linz
Susanne Titz, Director, Museum Abteiberg, Mönchengladbach

1   Will Bradley, 'Double Life', Frieze, Issue 105, March 2007, p. 149

Dieses Buch begleitet die bisher größte und umfangreichste Ausstellung des Werks von Cathy Wilkes. Die Ausstellung vereint jüngste Installationen mit Arbeiten, die fast ein Jahrzehnt zurückliegen, und dokumentiert damit die Vielfalt und die große Tiefe von Wilkes' Werk. Das Projekt ist dennoch keine klassische Retrospektive. Vielmehr werden hier Werke miteinander kombiniert und einander überlagert, bestimmte Elemente werden herausgegriffen und neu konfiguriert, um eine große Gesamtinstallation zu ergeben, die als eine neue eigene Arbeit erscheint, Fragmente aus verschiedenen Perioden von Wilkes' Arbeit in ein Gesamtkunstwerk überführt, das nur für die Dauer dieser Ausstellung und ihrer Tournee existiert. Bedeutende Installationen aus den letzten Jahren, darunter Untitled 2014 (Tramway, 2014) und Untitled (Possil, at last) 2013 (ursprünglich beauftragt für die 55. Biennale in Venedig), werden verbunden mit Elementen aus früheren Werken. In diesem Sinn nimmt das Display dieser Ausstellung jene Prinzipien von Installations- und Kombinationspraktiken auf, die Wilkes' Werk so spezifisch und eindringlich machen. Das Verständnis von räumlichen Beziehungen und der Bedeutung von An- und Abwesenheit in der Situation von Objekten zieht sich quer durch Wilkes' hochgradig durchdachtes und subtiles Werk. Betrachter sehen sich darin plötzlich in der Rolle eines Schauspielers, einer Schauspielerin, in einer Bewegung quer durch ein Bühnenbild. Oder vielleicht noch eher in der Rolle einer Archäologin oder eines Archäologen: Es könnten Ausgrabungen sein, die eine untergegangene Zivilisation entziffern, deren Mythologie, deren soziale und wirtschaftliche Strukturen.

Wilkes' Arbeiten sind oft als kompromisslos introspektiv beschrieben worden. Und tatsächlich sind ihre Installationen eindeutig verortet als Situationen: in Zeit und Raum, Geschehen auf einer linearen Karte von Ereignissen, die hier zu einer Zeitmaschine wird und dabei Autor wie Betrachter in eine bestimmte Zeit hinein führt. Sie alle entstammen aus Gedanken, Gefühlen, realen Situationen und emotionalen Zuständen bestimmter Abschnitte im Leben der Künstlerin. Die Konstellation der Objekte, deren Beziehungen und geheimnisvollen Evokationen, Darstellungen von Volumen oder Leeren, aus denen eigentlich Bühnenbilder entstehen, sind das Ergebnis (und die Erfüllung) einer großen Arbeit am Grundbestand von Affekten und Gedanken, eine Art Traumarbeit die sich hier dreidimensional entfaltet. Genau deswegen bedeutet eine Ausstellung, die Arbeiten aus verschiedenen Perioden der letzten Jahrzehnte in den Blick nimmt, für Wilkes ein Zurückgehen in vergangene Momente sowie auch das Aktivieren eines buchstäblich „retrospektiven Blicks", der die Werke nicht nur nochmals zeigt, sondern sie tatsächlich zu neuem Leben erweckt. Auch die Theatralität, die in Wilkes' Werk bereits während der 1990er Jahre und damit bemerkenswert früh galt und heute ein vielfach verwendeter Begriff in der Gegenwartskunst ist, wird mit diesem Konzept nochmals deutlicher sichtbar: Wenngleich die dargestellten Szenen eingefrorene Situationen sind, beginnt doch mit jedem neuen Aufbau das Theaterstück von neuem, kann sich die Szene ändern.

Die Erfahrung der „Neubelebung" ist hier nicht nur emotionale Erfahrung, sondern ein Teil von Wilkes' Ansatz. Ihre Arbeiten sind nicht notwendigerweise abgeschlossen und ab dem Zeitpunkt, da sie in die Welt geschickt werden, „in Stein gemeißelt". In der Tat sind gar nicht wenige von ihnen anlässlich weiterer Installationen modifiziert und überarbeitet worden. Die Installation Non Verbal, zum Beispiel, für die mehrere

Entstehungsdaten angegeben sind, gab es im Lauf der Zeit in mehreren verschiedenen Versionen. Das macht diese Arbeiten zu lebendigen Organismen, die sich nach ihren eigenen Gesetzen entwickeln und entsprechend den Veränderungen in ihrer Umgebung unter Umständen ausdehnen. Und während Museen normalerweise danach trachten, die Realität still zu stellen, um ein Objekt zu erhalten, das stabiler Gegenstand für die Erfahrung der künftigen Generationen wird, demonstriert diese Ausstellung die Instabilität von Wilkes' Praxis und zeigt in ihr die „Bedingung der Möglichkeit", im Sinn der Definition Immanuel Kants, der exakt diese Möglichkeit als eine notwendige Vorbedingung für die Erfahrung einer Entität (des ganzen Lebens) beschrieben hat. Dieser Ansatz bedeutet, dass wir das traditionelle Format einer Übersichtsschau verlassen haben, welche eine akribische Auswahl charakteristischer Objekte verlangt hätte, und stattdessen eine Ausstellung entstehen lassen wollten, die das repräsentiert, was Will Bradley als das Wesentliche für Wilkes' Arbeit identifiziert hat: „den Versuch, sich auf ein System von Objekten einzulassen im vollen Bewusstsein um die komplexen Bedeutungen und Beziehungen, die ein solches System hervorbringen kann".[1]

Diese Offenheit für Neubearbeitung ersetzt, sobald sie auf der Ebene des kuratorischen Prozesses wiederholt wird, die bloße Schaustellung der Vergangenheit durch deren Umschreiben und ermöglicht es, dabei Kunstgeschichte in Zeit und Raum kurzzuschließen. Die Trennlinie zwischen Werken unterschiedlicher Zeiten löst sich auf und ein Paralleluniversum entsteht, in dem Vergangenheit und Gegenwart simultan sind. Wilkes sagte einmal, dass für sie „Leben und Tod nicht getrennt sind" – die wechselseitige Durchdringung der Arbeiten, die sich in dieser Ausstellung ereignet, impliziert ein ganz ähnliches Begreifen von Grenzen als Schwellen, Türen, die man öffnen anstatt geschlossen halten sollte. Um die Elemente aus verschiedenen Epochen vorübergehend zu einer solchen Galaxie zusammenzufügen, ihr Gleichgewicht und gravitationelle Spannung zu geben, nutzt Wilkes in dieser Ausstellung anstelle der Wände Metallgitter und Wollfäden zur Befestigung von Objekten, formt sie zu einem organischen Gewebe. Diese Elemente haben zweierlei Funktion: Sie rahmen die einzelnen Werke und grenzen sie von einander ab, gleichzeitig können sie auch dazu dienen, disparate Elemente zu verknüpfen. Sie werden dabei zum Bild für das dreidimensionale Denken, lassen zudem das Licht durch die komplexe Struktur hindurch wandern.

Während der Konzeption dieses Projekts sagte Wilkes, was sie auch im ersten der beiden Texte tut, die sie in diesem Band publiziert: dass ihre Arbeit Mut zum Sehen machen solle. Es geht um die Intensität der dunklen Vorahnung, wenn wir irgendwo hinsehen, sie lenkt uns dorthin mittels einer Installation, die uns all die Urteile bewusst macht, die wir auf die Welt projizieren, noch bevor wir sie entziffert haben. Ihre Werke sind Konstruktionen, die eine sehr spezifische Art von Aufmerksamkeit erzeugen. Im Aufbau dieser Installationen halten sich Behinderung und Ermöglichung die Waage: Das Gefühl, dass in der Komposition ein Element fehlt, ist unter Umständen bewusst herbeigeführt, um eine Vorstellung von Verlust zu erzeugen. Diese Abwesenheit könnte die notwendige Instanz dafür sein, dass wir unsere Aufmerksamkeit neu schärfen, unsere Vorstellungskraft jenseits der Grenzen des Sichtbaren. Die Darstellung von Raum zwischen den Objekten kann dazu dienen, den Leerraum zu schaffen, den Bedeutung braucht, um in Erscheinung zu treten. Paradoxerweise ist Wilkes' Werk viel eher musikalisch als dreidimensional. Es bringt Wechsel mit sich, die die Erscheinung der Objekte verändern, aber auch die Zeit, in der der Blick der Betrachterinnen und Betrachter fluktuiert: ein Tanz, der die Kunstwerke sowohl mit den Sinnen wie mit dem Kopf dekodiert. Das Wachsen von Bedeutung und emotionaler Einfühlung ist das, was die Künstlerin von den Betrachtern verlangt. Sie macht es wie die Analytiker und zeigt einen Traum.

Um diesem einzigartigen Ansatz gerecht zu werden, der die Konventionen der klassischen Überblicksausstellung notwendigerweise unterminiert, ist die vorliegende Publikation kein herkömmlicher Katalog, sondern eher Karte und Begleiter, um näher an die Arbeitspraktiken und Denkprozesse von Cathy Wilkes zu führen. Das von der Künstlerin gemeinsam mit der Designerin Yvonne Quirmbach entworfene Buch bringt neue Texte, Detailfotos aus Installationen, Gemälde sowie auch neue Zeichnungen zusammen, die einige der in der Ausstellung behandelten Gedanken weiter ausbauen und entwickeln. Wie viele ihrer Projekte zuvor zeigt auch diese Ausstellung eine sorgsame Orchestrierung von Objekten, die sich letztlich als eine Verkettung erklärt. Die Publikation verfolgt diesen Gedanken, in ihrer rhythmischen Folge von Bildern und Leerstellen verweist sie auf wiederkehrende Motive und Beziehungen. Der Gleichklang zum Beispiel zwischen gemalten Äpfeln und dem Filzkopf einer Figur, die Spuren auf den gefundenen historischen Stoffen, die die Figuren bekleiden, und die Posen dieser Letztgenannten, die gründliche investigative Blicke herausfordern, sind nur einige der Verbindungsfäden, die in den visuellen und musikalischen Texten dieser Publikation auftauchen. Sie fungiert daher als eine Struktur, in der sich Wilkes' Praxis verstehen lässt als Film, der sich in den Dimensionen von Zeit und Raum entwickelt.

Cathy Wilkes wurde von dem ehemaligen leitenden Kurator der Tate Liverpool, Gavin Delahunty (heute Hoffman Family Senior Curator für moderne Kunst im Dallas Museum of Art) und der ehemaligen assistierenden Kuratorin Eleanor Clayton (heute Kuratorin in Hepworth Wakefield) eingeladen. Wir möchten ihnen beiden herzlich danken, ebenso wie auch dem engagierten Mitarbeiterteam der Tate Liverpool, insbesondere der Assistenzkuratorin Lauren Barnes für ihre unglaubliche Vision und Einsatzbereitschaft, die sie diesem Projekt gab, Tamsin Dillon als kommissarische Leitung der Ausstellungsabteilung sowie Sivan Amar (Registrar und Production Manager), Ken Simons (Art Handling Manager) und Barry Bentley (Deputy Art Handling Manager) für die Sorgfalt und Präzision, die sie einer derart komplexen Ausstellung gewidmet haben, sowie Jemima Pyne (Head of Media and Audiences) und Mike Pinnington (Content Editor) für ihre Unterstützung bei der Vermittlung dieses Projekts an unser Publikum. Anders als bei einer typischen Wanderausstellung wird die Präsentation der Ausstellung an jedem Ort gemeinsam mit der Künstlerin noch einmal neu konzipiert und in Beziehung zum veränderten Kontext in Szene gesetzt. Im Lentos Kunstmuseum möchten wir dem ganzen engagierten Team danken, insbesondere Magnus Hofmüller (Produktionsleiter), Andreas Strohhammer (Restaurator), Milena Dimitrova (Registrarin), Dunja Schneider (Leitung Kunstvermittlung) und Nina Kirsch (Presse). Im Museum Abteiberg danken wir ebenfalls allen

Kolleginnen und Kollegen für die Einsatzbereitschaft und Sorgfalt, mit der sie den Aufbau dieser Ausstellung begleiten, ein besonderer Dank gilt Christine Adolphs (Restaurierung), Achim Hirdes (Ausstellungstechnik) und ihrem Installationsteam.

Wir danken herzlich allen öffentlichen Museen und Privatpersonen, die uns so großzügig Werke aus ihren Kollektionen für die Ausstellung in Liverpool, Linz und Mönchengladbach geliehen haben, insbesondere der Rennie Collection, die zudem die Ausstellung selbst unterstützte. Die Ausstellung in der Tate Liverpool wurde gefördert von der Henry Moore Foundation, Culture Ireland und dem British Council Northern Ireland, auch ihnen allen gilt herzlicher Dank. Die Ausstellung in Liverpool wurde ermöglicht durch das Indemnity Scheme der britischen Regierung. Die Tate Liverpool dankt der britischen Regierung für die Bereitstellung des Versicherungsschutzes der Werke sowie dem Ministerium für Kultur, Medien und Sport und dem Arts Council England für dessen Organisation. Das Museum Abteiberg möchte seinen tiefen Dank gegenüber den institutionellen Förderern, der Kunststiftung NRW und der Hans Fries-Stiftung aussprechen, welche die Ausstellung in Mönchengladbach ermöglicht haben.

Wir danken Yvonne Quirmbach für ihren kreativen und höchst kooperativen Ansatz in der Gestaltung dieser Publikation. Sie hat eng mit Cathy Wilkes zusammengearbeitet, um ein Buch zu schaffen, das den eigenen Ideen dieser außergewöhnlichen Künstlerin in perfekter Weise folgt. Ferner möchten wir uns insbesondere bei Toby Webster und Xavier Hufkens für ihre großzügige Unterstützung dieser Publikation bedanken. Außerdem gilt Dank den Teams des Modern Institute und Xavier Hufkens, die so effizient und unermüdlich bei vielen entscheidenden Aspekten der Ausstellung und des Buchs mitgeholfen haben. Ein ganz großes Dankeschön an Darren Rhymes, der als Assistent von Cathy Wilkes das Projekt von Anfang bis Ende mit größter Sorgfalt und Aufmerksamkeit betreute. Und zuletzt bedanken wir uns zutiefst Cathy Wilkes selbst. Die Gelegenheit, an ihrer Welt teilzuhaben für die Zeit der gemeinsamen Arbeit war ein großes Privileg. Wir sind glücklich darüber, dass wir diese Erfahrung nunmehr durch eine Ausstellung und ein Buch mit Anderen teilen können.

Andrea Nixon, Executive Director, Tate Liverpool
Francesco Manacorda, Artistic Director, Tate Liverpool
Stella Rollig, Direktorin, Lentos Kunstmuseum Linz
Susanne Titz, Direktorin, Museum Abteiberg, Mönchengladbach

1   Will Bradley, „Double Life", Frieze, Nr. 105, März 2007, S. 149.

PLATES
ABBILDUNGEN

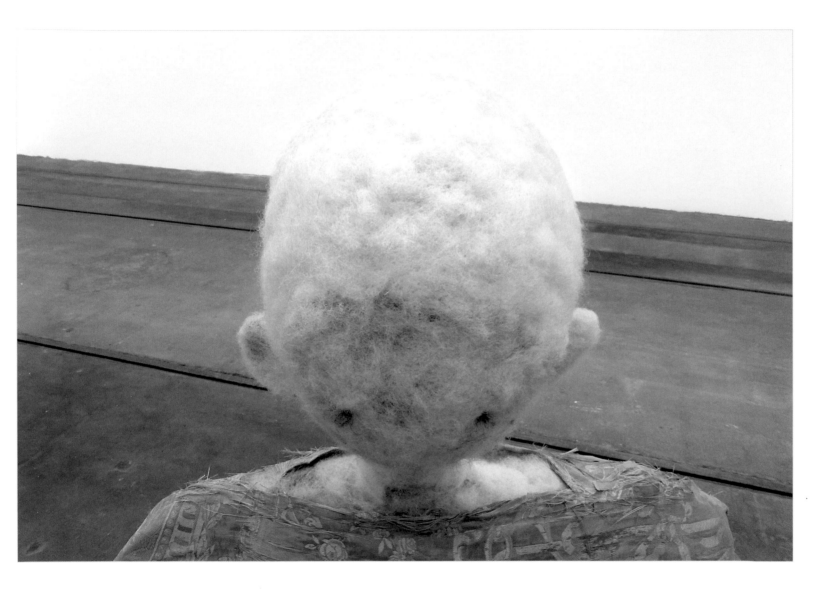

Er kletterte hinauf, um die Menschenmenge zu überblicken, da er klein von Wuchs war.
Er sagte,
„Es gibt hier niemand, der mehr als acht Pfund in der Stunde wert ist."
Das war das Geheimnis, das er sich selbst offenbarte. Er suchte sofort danach, sobald
er sah, dass die Menschen sich versammelt hatten. Sein Atmen und das Schlagen seines
Herzens störten den Ort, und er gehorchte ihnen. Vor sich konnte er bloß die Kräfte
der Natur und ein dem Tod Nahesein sehen.
Er wusste es und er sagte,
"Wenn ich verschwinden könnte, dann werden die Menschen, die ich dort vor mir
sehe, in Schönheit vollkommen werden, schon deshalb, weil ich sie nicht mit meinen
Anhäufungen und meinen Sinnen verdecke. In Omoa sah ich eine Frau auf der Straße,
überzogen mit der roten und gelben Glasur, mitten in einem Unwetter aus Wind und
Wasser. Unsere Bevölkerung ist so spärlich und so voll Tatkraft.
Als ich jung war, verwendete ich die Materialien, die Du mir gegeben hast.
Ich gestalte den ganzen Vorgang des Produzierens und Schaffens feierlich, sogar in
meinem göttlichen Obstgarten. Das triefnasse Gras unter meinen beiden bloßen Füßen.
Ich gebe meinen Schöpfungen Würde auf der anderen Seite des Vorhangs. Bei welcher
Gelegenheit könnte ich in einer solchen Stille sein?"
Am Anfang war die Vermittlung und die Vermittlung war bei Gott und die Vermittlung
war Gott. Dasselbe war am Anfang bei Gott. Alle Dinge wurden daraus gemacht und
ohne es wurde nichts gemacht, was gemacht wurde.

He climbed up to see over the crowd of people because he was small in stature. He said,
"There's nobody here worth more than eight pounds an hour."
That was the secret which he revealed to himself. He searched for it immediately when he saw the people assembled. His breathing and the beating of his heart disturbed the place and he obeyed them. In front of him he could see only the forces of nature and a proximity to death.
He knew it and he said,
"If I could disappear, the people I see there before me will become perfect in beauty from the very fact that I do not obscure them with my accumulations and my senses. In Omoa I saw a woman in the road, covered in the red and yellow glazes, in the midst of a tempest of wind and water. Our population is so thinly scattered and so enterprising.
When I was young I used the materials thou hast given to me. I solemnise all the producing and creating, even in my divine orchard. The soaking grass under my two bare feet. I dignify my creations on the other side of the curtain. On what occasion might I be in such a silence?"
In the beginning was the Mediation and the Mediation was with God and the Mediation was God. The same was in the beginning with God. All things were made of it and without it was not anything made that was made.

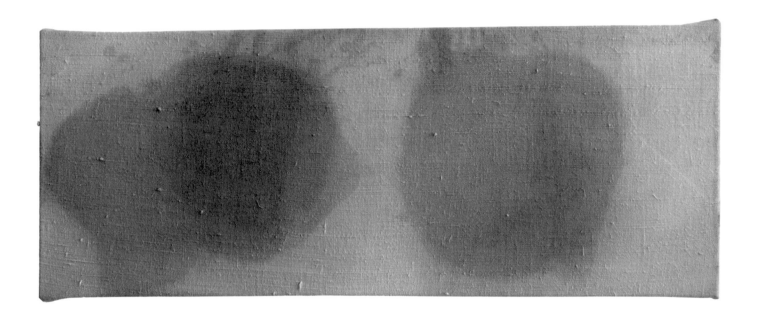

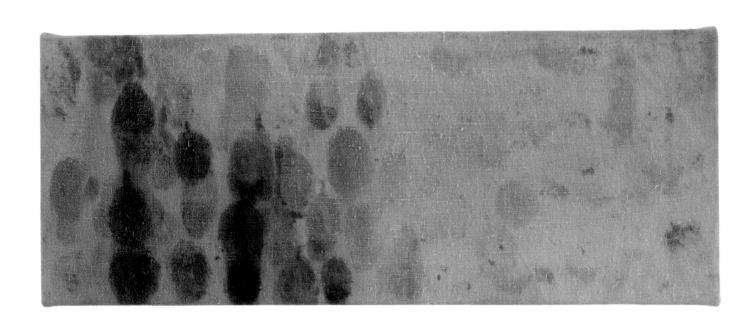

Welche Kraft es mir gab, deine liebe E-Mail vorzufinden, als ich gestern Abend nach Hause kam! Ich konnte das Ticken deiner Uhr irgendwo ganz nahe hören.

Allmählich und jetzt ganz und gar wirst du plötzlich den furchtbaren Schlamm und das Wasser sehen. Du wirst sie alle ertrunken vorfinden, wie sie mit dem Rücken nach oben darin treiben, alle gleich, mit dem aufgeblasenen blauen Stoff ihrer Hosen, sie alle direkt vor dir und die scheußlichen Riffe aus Schlamm. Davor ist die Steppe mit ihren Kalksteinkieseln, gelb und grau, soweit das Auge reicht.

Ich hab noch immer dasselbe Haus und alles ist, wie es war. Ich hab gewartet und mich gefragt, ob du sehr krank oder schmerzerfüllt bist. Warst du im Gefängnis? Die Nachbarin hat mir gesagt, das sei der Grund.

So very sustaining to receive your kind email when I returned last night!
I could hear the tick of your watch somewhere near.
Little by little and now all together, all at once you'll see all the terrible
mud and water. You'll see them all drowned, with their backs floating in it,
all alike with the blue cloth of their trousers blown up in the very place
where you are, and there are horrible reefs of mud. In front there is the
chalky pebbled steppe, yellow and grey as far as the eye can see.
I have the same house and everything is the same here. I was waiting and
I wondered if you were very ill or full of anguish. Were you in prison?
The neighbour said to me that was the reason.

Northern

DUNDONALD BRANCH
971 UPPER NEWTOWNARDS ROAD
BELFAST BT16 0RL NORTHERN IRELAND

For 24 hour banking call 08457 365 024

95-01-25

Date 20 07 05

Pay CATHY WILKES or order

One hundred & fifty pounds

£ 150—00

G T WILKES

NORTHERN BANK LIMITED
08FEB05

DLRS APACS 9552

Cheque No.   Sort Code   Account No.

⑈200845⑈ 95⑈0125⑈ 91010476⑈02

12: <u>Untitled / Ohne Titel</u>, 2012, mixed media / Mischtechnik, dimensions variable / Abmessungen variabel, The Modern Institute, Glasgow, 2012, Rennie Collection, courtesy of the artist and / mit freundlicher Genehmigung der Künstlerin und The Modern Institute/Toby Webster Ltd, Glasgow, Photo Ruth Clark · 13: <u>Untitled / Ohne Titel</u>, 2012, mixed media / Mischtechnik, dimensions variable / Abmessungen variabel, The Modern Institute, Glasgow, 2012, Rennie Collection, courtesy of the artist and / mit freundlicher Genehmigung der Künstlerin und The Modern Institute/Toby Webster Ltd, Glasgow, Photo Ruth Clark · 17, 19, 21, 23: <u>Untitled (Possil, at last) / Ohne Titel (endlich Possil)</u>, 2013, mixed media / Mischtechnik, dimensions variable / Abmessungen variabel, 'The Encyclopedic Palace', Venice Biennale / 'Der enzyklopädische Palast', Biennale Venedig, 2013, Tate: Purchased / Ankauf 2014, courtesy of the artist and / mit freundlicher Genehmigung der Künstlerin und The Modern Institute/Toby Webster Ltd, Glasgow, Photo Cristiano Corte · 25: <u>Untitled / Ohne Titel</u>, 2013, mixed media / Mischtechnik, dimensions variable / Abmessungen variabel, Xavier Hufkens, Brussels, 2013, Private Collection / Privatbesitz, Brussels, courtesy of the artist and / mit freundlicher Genehmigung der Künstlerin und Xavier Hufkens, Brussels / Brüssel, Photo Allard Bovenberg, Amsterdam · 27, 29: <u>Untitled / Ohne Titel</u>, 2014, mixed media / Mischtechnik, dimensions variable / Abmessungen variabel, Tramway, Glasgow, 2014, Collection of / Sammlung Museum of Modern Art, Warsaw, courtesy of the artist and / mit freundlicher Genehmigung der Künstlerin und The Modern Institute/Toby Webster Ltd, Glasgow, Photo Darren Rhymes · 31, 33: <u>Untitled / Ohne Titel</u>, 2014, mixed media / Mischtechnik, dimensions variable / Abmessungen variabel, Tramway, Glasgow, 2014, Collection of / Sammlung Museum Museum of Modern Art, Warsaw, courtesy of the artist and / mit freundlicher Genehmigung der Künstlerin und The Modern Institute/Toby Webster Ltd, Glasgow, Photo Keith Hunter · 35: <u>Untitled (Possil, at last) / Ohne Titel (endlich Possil)</u>, 2013, mixed media / Mischtechnik, dimensions variable / Abmessungen variabel, 'The Encyclopedic Palace', Venice Biennale / 'Der enzyklopädische Palast', Biennale Venedig, 2013, Tate: Purchased / Ankauf 2014, courtesy of the artist and / mit freundlicher Genehmigung der Künstlerin und The Modern Institute/Toby Webster Ltd, Glasgow, Photo Cristiano Corte · 39: <u>Untitled / Ohne Titel</u>, 2013, oil paint on linen / Öl auf Leinwand, 31 x 77 x 3 cm, Wassim Rasamny Collection / Sammlung, courtesy of the artist and / mit freundlicher Genehmigung der Künstlerin und Xavier Hufkens, Brussels / Brüssel, Photo Allard Bovenberg, Amsterdam · 40: <u>Untitled / Ohne Titel</u>, 2012, oil paint on linen/ Öl auf Leinwand, 18.5 x 25.5 x 1.5 cm, Collection of / Sammlung Dr. Roberta and Mr. Sheldon Toll, courtesy of the artist and / mit freundlicher Genehmigung der Künstlerin und The Modern Institute/Toby Webster Ltd, Glasgow, Photo Brian Forrest · 41: <u>Untitled / Ohne Titel</u>, 2012, oil paint on linen / Öl auf Leinwand, 26 x 36 x 2 cm, Rennie Collection, courtesy of the artist and / mit freundlicher Genehmigung der Künstlerin und The Modern Institute/Toby Webster Ltd, Glasgow, Photo Ruth Clark · 43: <u>Untitled / Ohne Titel</u>, 2012, oil paint on linen / Öl auf Leinwand, 26 x 36 x 2 cm, Rennie Collection, courtesy of the artist and / mit freundlicher Genehmigung der Künstlerin und The Modern Institute/Toby Webster Ltd, Glasgow, Photo Ruth Clark · 45: <u>Untitled / Ohne Titel</u>, 2012, oil paint on linen / Öl auf Leinwand, 18 x 25 x 2 cm, Private Collection / Privatsammlung Toby Webster, Glasgow, courtesy of the artist and /

mit freundlicher Genehmigung der Künstlerin und The Modern Institute/Toby Webster Ltd, Glasgow, Photo Ruth Clark · 46: <u>Untitled / Ohne Titel</u>, 2013, oil paint on linen / Öl auf Leinwand, 18 x 25 x 2 cm, Private Collection / Privatbesitz, London, courtesy of the artist and / mit freundlicher Genehmigung der Künstlerin und The Modern Institute/Toby Webster Ltd, Glasgow, Photo Dawn Blackman · 47: <u>Untitled / Ohne Titel</u>, 2012, oil paint on linen / Öl auf Leinwand, 25.5 x 37 x 2 cm, Rennie Collection, courtesy of the artist and / mit freundlicher Genehmigung der Künstlerin und The Modern Institute/Toby Webster Ltd, Glasgow, Photo Blaine Campbell · 49: <u>Untitled / Ohne Titel</u>, 2013, oil paint on linen / Öl auf Leinwand, 25.5 x 36.5 x 1.5 cm, Private Collection / Privatbesitz, Brussels, courtesy of the artist and / mit freundlicher Genehmigung der Künstlerin und Xavier Hufkens, Brussels / Brüssel, Photo Allard Bovenberg, Amsterdam · 51: <u>Untitled / Ohne Titel</u>, 2013, oil paint on linen / Öl auf Leinwand, 21 x 51 x 2 cm, Private Collection / Privatbesitz, Brussels, courtesy of the artist and / mit freundlicher Genehmigung der Künstlerin und Xavier Hufkens, Brussels / Brüssel, Photo Allard Bovenberg, Amsterdam · 60: <u>Untitled / Ohne Titel</u>, 2015, pastel on paper / Pastell auf Papier, 30 x 44 cm, courtesy of the artist and / mit freundlicher Genehmigung der Künstlerin und The Modern Institute/Toby Webster Ltd, Glasgow · 61: <u>Untitled / Ohne Titel</u>, 2015, pastel on paper / Pastell auf Papier, 30 x 44 cm, courtesy of the artist and / mit freundlicher Genehmigung der Künstlerin und The Modern Institute/Toby Webster Ltd, Glasgow · 62: <u>Untitled / Ohne Titel</u>, 2015, pastel on paper / Pastell auf Papier, 30 x 44 cm, courtesy of the artist and / mit freundlicher Genehmigung der Künstlerin und The Modern Institute/Toby Webster Ltd, Glasgow · 63: <u>Untitled / Ohne Titel</u>, 2015, pastel on paper / Pastell auf Papier, 30 x 44 cm, courtesy of the artist and / mit freundlicher Genehmigung der Künstlerin und The Modern Institute/Toby Webster Ltd, Glasgow

First published 2015 by order of the Tate Trustees by Tate Liverpool on the occasion of the exhibition
Erstmals veröffentlicht 2015 im Auftrag der Tate Trustees von Tate Liverpool anlässlich der Ausstellung
CATHY WILKES
Tate Liverpool, 06.03.–31.05.2015 · Lentos Kunstmuseum Linz, 03.07.–04.10.2015 · Museum Abteiberg, Mönchengladbach, 08.11.2015–14.02.2016

Publication supported by / Publikation unterstützt von: The Modern Institute/Toby Webster Ltd, Glasgow · Xavier Hufkens, Brussels / Brüssel
Exhibition supported by / Ausstellung unterstützt von: Rennie Collection · The Henry Moore Foundation · Culture Ireland ·
British Council Northern Ireland · Arts Foundation of North Rhine-Westphalia / Kunststiftung NRW

ISBN 978-1-84976-345-5

Text by / von: Cathy Wilkes · Design by / von: Yvonne Quirmbach · Printed by / Gedruckt von: Medialis Offsetdruck GmbH, Berlin

Tate Liverpool, Albert Dock, Liverpool Waterfront, L3 4BB, United Kingdom / Großbritannien, tate.org.uk
LENTOS Kunstmuseum Linz, Ernst-Koref-Promenade 1, 4020 Linz, Austria / Österreich, lentos.at
Museum Abteiberg, Abteistraße 27, D-41061 Mönchengladbach, Germany / Deutschland, museum-abteiberg.de

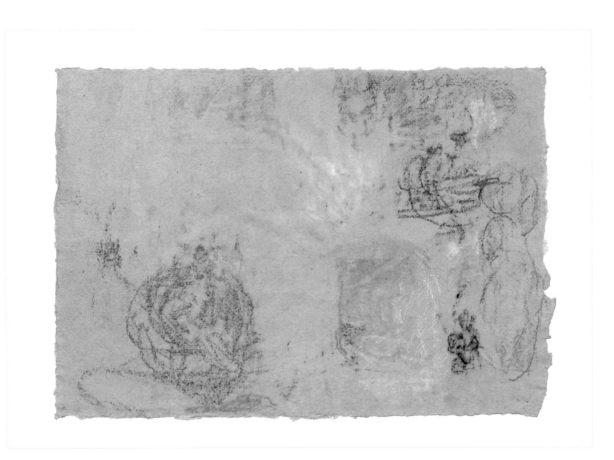